Report by the
Comptroller and Auditor General

Revenue from
Gambling Duties

Ordered by the
House of Commons
to be printed 27 March 2000

LONDON: The Stationery Office
£9.25

HC 352 Session 1999-2000
Published 30 March 2000

This report has been prepared under Section 6 of the National Audit Act 1983 for presentation to the House of Commons in accordance with Section 9 of the Act.

John Bourn Comptroller and Auditor General	National Audit Office 9 March 2000

The Comptroller and Auditor General is the head of the National Audit Office employing some 750 staff. He, and the National Audit Office, are totally independent of Government. He certifies the accounts of all Government departments and a wide range of other public sector bodies; and he has statutory authority to report to Parliament on the economy, efficiency and effectiveness with which departments and other bodies have used their resources.

For further information about the National Audit Office please contact:

National Audit Office
Press Office
157-197 Buckingham Palace Road
Victoria
London
SW1W 9SP

Tel: 020-7798 7400

email: enquiries@nao.gsi.gov.uk

Web site address: www.nao.gov.uk

Contents

Appendices

Cover photograph reproduced by kind permission of Rank Leisure, Grosvenor Casinos.

Executive summary

1   There are six types of gambling duties including those on the National Lottery, pools betting, bingo, gaming such as casinos, general betting (such as bets taken by bookmakers), and licences to operate individual amusement machines. In 1998-99 HM Customs and Excise (the Department) collected £1,530 million in gambling duties; an increase of some 22 per cent in real terms over the amount collected in 1993-94. The amount of duties collected in 1998-99 represented an average rate of 22 per cent of the £7 billion spent on gambling in the United Kingdom, which was approximately 1.3 per cent of total consumer expenditure or £284 for every household.

2   This report examines:

  ■ the Department's analysis and management of risks to the revenue;

  ■ whether the Department's arrangements for deploying their resources are fully effective in meeting the risks.

3   Our review of gambling duties has been carried out in parallel with a review of the work of the Gaming Board examining their role in regulating the gambling industry. This work was co-ordinated so that the findings could be compared and areas identified for greater co-operation that could improve performance. A report on the Gaming Board is due to be published shortly.

The Department's analysis and management of risks to the revenue

Identifying the risk

4   The Department are responsible for assessing whether traders have paid the correct amount of duty and for detecting and deterring illegal traders who are seeking to evade duties. Responses from the Department's 13 collections show that the highest risks to gambling revenue are:

  ■ operators using amusement machines without obtaining licences which were cited by eleven collections;

  ■ illegal bookmakers which were mentioned by ten collections.

Most collections' effort was devoted to auditing the highest risks to the revenue, amusement machine suppliers and operators and bookmakers. On the other duties the collections generally perceived the risks to revenue to be lower.

5　For amusement machines, unlike other betting and gaming duties, there is no statutory requirement for licensing authorities to notify the Department of traders eligible to pay the licence duties. The Department recognise that there is a risk that they may not be aware of all permitted sites or operators and that consequently duty on some amusement machine licences may not be collected.

6　There are over 200,000 machines where the licence can be purchased either by one of some 850 suppliers, or major operators or by over 60,000 small operators of the machines. Legislation is silent as to whether the supplier or the operator of amusement machine purchases the licence. The Department recognise that there may be some benefits if the 850 or so amusement machine suppliers were made responsible for purchasing the licenses.

7　Apart from amusement machines, the main way by which the Department becomes aware of a new trader undertaking betting and gaming activities is through the local licensing authorities. As there are over 1,000 licensing authorities in the United Kingdom giving an average of almost 77 licensing authorities for each collection, there is a risk that these licensing authorities may be uncertain to which of the Department's 13 collections they should report details of new traders. A licensing authority may, therefore, not always inform a collection of all new traders and the situation may not be detected by the collection.

8　The placing of telephone bets through bookmakers that are based offshore and betting and gaming on the Internet could substantially affect the amounts of revenue that the Department collect in duties in the future. The Department estimate that lost revenue from telephone betting would amount to £50 million in 2000-2001 if all telephone betting was to move offshore. Because betting and gaming on the Internet is still developing the Department estimate that the amount of revenue that is currently lost is only small but they recognise it as a growing threat.

Information on illegal traders

9　There is only a limited amount of information available within the Department that might alert officers to the probability of illegal trading and they mainly rely on intelligence to identify the possibility of its occurrence. Three cost-effective ways the Department obtains information on potential illegal traders are:

■ through the use of hot lines which are published within local telephone directories and on the Department's web site but not the Yellow Pages. Due to the cost of advertising space in the numerous local directories, the Department have confined the advertising of the hotline to reporting illegal activities concerned with drug smuggling and VAT evasion. The Department are considering, however, the possibility of including more information in the directories and whether it will be cost effective to do so. The Department's web site only mentions illegal betting;

■ contacts with registered traders such as major bookmakers who have introduced their own teams to detect illegal bookmakers, usually operating in premises, such as public houses, which are not licensed for gambling;

■ sharing information with other public sector organisations who have an interest in the activities of illegal traders. Collections have occasionally obtained information from the police and the Gaming Board and the Inland Revenue, making use of the statutory provision allowing HM Customs and Excise to obtain information from the Inland Revenue to assist with their duties. This information has helped the Department increase their understanding of the risks of illegal trading in their areas.

Actions against illegal traders

10 From 1995-96 to 1998-99, there were 18 cases where the Department took criminal action with respect to unlicensed amusement machines and 74 civil prosecutions. In addition 841 machines were seized leading to £206,000 of restitution receipts. Although there is no requirement on amusement machines operators to pay arrears of duties on machines for periods of illegal operation, action by the Department was nevertheless successful in collecting duty of £380,000 or £4,130 per case.

11 If the Department finds that a supplier is not er uring that amusement machine licences are being purchased they may pass the information to the Gaming Board. The Board take into account the licensing of machines and will consider withdrawing certificates to trade from any supplier that incurs civil or criminal penalties. The Department are currently seeking to improve their arrangements for sharing information with the Gaming Board and our work confirmed that there is scope for the Department to work more closely with The Board, to tighten controls.

12 From 1995-96 to 1998-99, there were 26 cases where the Department took criminal proceedings against illegal bookmakers and 15 cases of civil proceedings. The rate of return was relatively low with total duty charged amounting to £175,000, an average of £4,300 per case.

Recommendations

13 On the Department's methods and information for dealing with the main risks to the revenue we have made a number of detailed recommendations (paragraph 2.27). Key recommendations are that the Department should:

- improve their procedures with respect to information from licensing authorities and their own records of licensed traders;

- look at whether they should pursue amusement machine operators for arrears of duty during periods of illegal operation;

- in assessing risk across excise duties, ensure that they still pursue sufficient cases of illegal bookmaking in order to maintain the integrity of the duty;

- improve methods of obtaining intelligence on illegal traders such as by giving wider publicity to their hot line and sharing information with other agencies on illegal traders.

Deploying resources to meet the risks to revenue

Allocating staff

14 The Department allocate staff resources to collections for the audit of traders paying excise duties generally, rather than specifically for the audit of gambling duties. In 1998-99, total staff resources for excise duties were 1,400 staff years. Of this total, collections allocated some 41 staff years to the audit of gambling traders at a cost of £1.4 million. From 2000-2001 the Department will allocate resources according to a new risk model. The results of their risk assessment to date show that there are imbalances in the deployment of resources between collections and that it may be possible to reduce the numbers auditing excise traders, including betting and gaming and redeploy them to deal with other risks to the revenue. The Department intend to redistribute staff between collections gradually as they recognise that the risk assessment work needs to be refined based on further experience and more data.

15 The Department intend to select for audit a percentage of the traders from each risk category designated low, medium and high which will range from 25 percent to 100 percent of excise and inland customs traders. Teams within each collection will sift the traders selected and pass to assurance staff those traders they assess as being potentially non compliant. Because the Department's approach applies to all traders paying excise duties, there are risks that individual duties such as gambling could receive little attention if these traders are not selected for audit. The Department intend to monitor whether there has been sufficient audit coverage of individual duties and will increase coverage if necessary.

Setting targets and measuring performance

16 The Department have set general targets for additional revenue collected from excise traders and forecasts of revenue from gambling traders. These targets do not relate resources used to the level of under declaration. As currently designed, this could lead to over concentration on a few high risk traders with insufficient information being available on the overall levels of compliance and accuracy in the collection of gambling duties. From April 2000, the Department intend to introduce a new measure which will relate the level of resources used to the amount of additional revenue discovered.

Efficient use of staff

17 The Department recognise that when they introduce their new system for allocating staff to collections they will need to monitor how collections then allocate their staff to audit work. In particular the Department need to assess the extent to which collections are focusing on the areas of highest risk suggested by the risk assessment exercise and whether the results from the risk assessment exercise are robust.

18 Collections organise their staff using either a "centralised" or "dispersed" approach and we analysed each of the Department's 13 collections according to their approach. The results of our analysis indicated that the effectiveness of the centralised approach is significantly greater in terms of the value of errors detected per officer year.

Developing good practice

19 The Department's three Centres of Operational Expertise are responsible for improving professionalism within the Department and identifying and developing good practices in auditing traders in betting and gaming. They cover three of the gambling duties (general betting, amusement machine licence duty and gaming duty). On our visits to collections staff mentioned that although the Centres are helpful in providing advice when contacted, they do not take a proactive approach in disseminating information and good practice. The Department have carried out a review of the roles and responsibilities of the centres for all duties including gambling. As a result the Department intend to set up one centre covering all gambling duties and they are considering whether there is more that the centre could do to identify and disseminate good practice.

20 The Department recognises that sharing information with other organisations can be an efficient and effective way of supplementing the information they hold on a traders activities. In order to explore the opportunities for closer working and sharing of information we set up a joint meeting with representatives of the Department and the Gaming Board. This identified areas where there could be greater co-operation such as two way secondments, and sharing information on traders.

Recommendations

21 In deploying resources to meet the risks to the revenue, we have made a number of detailed recommendations (paragraph 3.33). The key recommendations are that the Department should:

- ensure that sufficient audit coverage is given to each individual duty within each financial year;

- consider whether Collections have organised their staff resources in the most efficient way to carry out audit work on betting and gaming traders;

- conduct sufficient random audits and set appropriate audit targets to measure the results of betting and gaming work;

- ensure that the Centres of Expertise are proactive in disseminating information and good practice on auditing traders; and

■ take forward the opportunities identified for closer co-operation with the Gaming Board and other organisations including the Horserace Betting Levy Board and the Tote.

Part 1: Introduction

Public bodies with responsibilities for the gambling industry

1.1 The Department is one of eight groups of public bodies with responsibilities for the gambling industry (Figure 1). Our review of gambling duties has been carried out in parallel with a review of the Gaming Board examining their role in regulating the gambling industry. This work was co-ordinated so that the findings could be compared and areas identified for greater co-operation that could improve performance. A report on the Gaming Board is due to be published shortly.

1.2 The main controls on the gambling industry are laid down in three Acts of Parliament - the Betting, Gaming and Lotteries Act 1963, the Gaming Act 1968 and the Lotteries and Amusement Act 1976 and associated secondary legislation. In December 1999, the Home Office announced that an independent review body would be established in 2000 to design a new regulatory structure for the gambling industry and to test public opinion. In setting up the review the Home Office recognise that social attitudes to gambling have changed and that the law is being overtaken by technological developments. Their aim is to remove unnecessary burdens on business while maintaining protections which are in the public interest.

HM Customs and Excise objectives with respect to gambling duties

1.3 Each year the Department publish a top-level statement of their objectives and targets which are supported internally by detailed plans. In 1998-99 the Department's aim was to improve the revenue yield from indirect taxes and safeguard the integrity of the taxes and duties. The aim applies to all taxes collected by the Department including gambling duties. Specific objectives that are relevant to gambling duties are:

■ to collect the forecast revenue;

■ to improve compliance by ensuring the accuracy of trader's declarations by carrying out a risk based assurance programme; and

■ to provide assurance that the Departmental registers accurately reflect the details of all taxable or authorised persons.

Figure 1

The responsibilities of the main public sector bodies with a role in the activities of the gambling industry

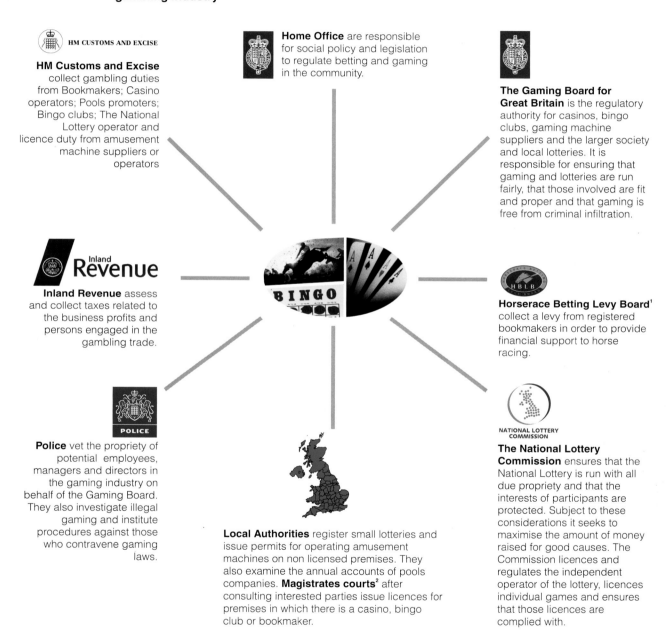

HM CUSTOMS AND EXCISE

HM Customs and Excise collect gambling duties from Bookmakers; Casino operators; Pools promoters; Bingo clubs; The National Lottery operator and licence duty from amusement machine suppliers or operators

Home Office are responsible for social policy and legislation to regulate betting and gaming in the community.

The Gaming Board for Great Britain is the regulatory authority for casinos, bingo clubs, gaming machine suppliers and the larger society and local lotteries. It is responsible for ensuring that gaming and lotteries are run fairly, that those involved are fit and proper and that gaming is free from criminal infiltration.

Inland Revenue

Inland Revenue assess and collect taxes related to the business profits and persons engaged in the gambling trade.

Horserace Betting Levy Board[1] collect a levy from registered bookmakers in order to provide financial support to horse racing.

POLICE

Police vet the propriety of potential employees, managers and directors in the gaming industry on behalf of the Gaming Board. They also investigate illegal gaming and institute procedures against those who contravene gaming laws.

NATIONAL LOTTERY COMMISSION

The National Lottery Commission ensures that the National Lottery is run with all due propriety and that the interests of participants are protected. Subject to these considerations it seeks to maximise the amount of money raised for good causes. The Commission licences and regulates the independent operator of the lottery, licences individual games and ensures that those licences are complied with.

Local Authorities register small lotteries and issue permits for operating amusement machines on non licensed premises. They also examine the annual accounts of pools companies. **Magistrates courts**[2] after consulting interested parties issue licences for premises in which there is a casino, bingo club or bookmaker.

Note: 1. The Home Office announced on 2 March 2000 that the Board and Levy are to be abolished.

2. Licensing Committee of the local authority in Scotland

Source: National Audit Office

The Department's organisational structure for gambling duties

1.4 The Department separate their activities with respect to gambling duties between (Figure 2):

a) the **Operational Compliance Directorate**, which sets operational policy and performance targets, allocates resources to collections and provides general guidance and training;

b) the **Excise Policy Group**, which is responsible for legislation and policy covering betting and gaming taxes and for providing advice and support to Treasury ministers on betting and gaming taxation matters;

c) **Accounting operations**, which accounts for traders' duty returns - receipts from pool betting duty, are collected and accounted for in Liverpool, and betting and gaming duties are collected and accounted for in Greenock;

The Department's organisational structure for gambling duties

Figure 2

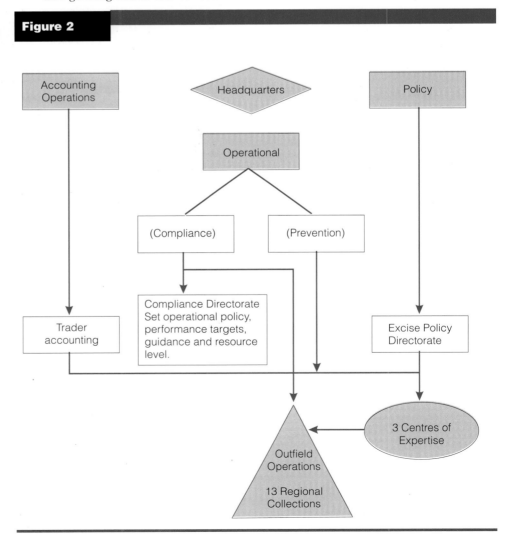

Source: National Audit Office

d) thirteen regional **Executive units or Collections**, which are responsible for carrying out audits on traders located within their areas to ensure compliance; and

e) three **Centres of Operational Expertise** (COPEs), which are responsible for assisting in development and implementation of policy; improving professionalism within the Department; and operational effectiveness, for example by identifying and developing good practices in auditing betting and gaming traders. The centres are based in Collections; Eastern England is responsible for betting duty, London Central for casinos and North West England for amusement machine licences.

Current rates of gambling duties

Gaming Duty is payable on the total stake less players winnings where the club is banker plus table money where the bank is shared by players

Photograph by kind permission of Rank Leisure, Grosvenor Casinos

1.5 The Betting and Gaming Duties Act 1981, as amended by subsequent Finance Acts, provides for gambling duties to be collected by the Department. The legislation defines the circumstances in which each of the duties is payable (Appendix A). Pools duty, introduced in 1948, was the first tax on gambling in the post war era. There are now six types of gambling duty out of a total of over 40 excise duties. They are duties on the National Lottery, pools betting, bingo, gaming such as casinos, general betting (such as bets taken by bookmakers), and licences to operate individual amusement machines. Some betting and gaming activities are not subject to duty. For example, cash bets taken by on course bookmakers; bingo promoted by an all member club or small-scale bingo played at travelling fairs; and local lotteries which are operated for charitable purposes. Figure 3 sets out the current rates of duties.

The current rates of gambling duty

Figure 3

Duty	Type of Duty	Rate of Duty
National Lottery	Percentage of amount staked	12%
General Betting	Percentage of amount staked	6.75%
Bingo	Percentage of weekly stake and added prize money	10% of the price of the bingo card plus 1/9th of added prize money
Pool Betting	Percentage of amount staked	17.5%
Gaming duty	A premises based tax on banded profits	2.5% to 40% stepped increases
Amusement Machine Licence	Licence for each manchine or for premises based on machines in use	Licence value £250, £645 or £1,815 per annum dependent on machine type and cost per play

Source: HM Customs & Excise

Receipts from gambling duties

Most amusement machines require a licence when they are being used

Photograph by kind permission of Gillman and Soame

1.6 In 1998-99, the Department collected £1,530 million in gambling duties; an increase of some 22 per cent over the £1,256 million, (in real terms), of gambling duties collected in 1993-94 (Figure 4a). During this period gambling duties collected have provided some 1.6 per cent of the total annual revenue, including VAT, collected by the Department. In 1998-99, this represented an average rate of 22 per cent of the £7 billion net amount spent on gambling in the United Kingdom, which was nearly 1.3 per cent of consumer expenditure or £284 for every household (Figure 4b) and Appendix B.

1.7 Between 1993-94 and 1998-99, the following key changes in revenue have arisen (Figure 4a):

a) total betting and gaming receipts have increased by 22 percent, in real terms predominantly because the National Lottery, introduced in November 1994, yielded £628 million in 1998-99, or some 41 per cent of the total duties collected from betting and gaming;

Betting and Gaming duties collected between 1993-94 and 1998-99

Figure 4a

The introduction of the lottery has increased the overall revenue from betting and gaming

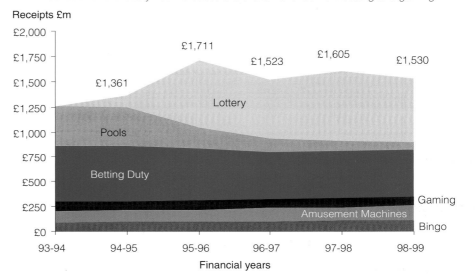

Receipts £m

£1,361   £1,711   £1,523   £1,605   £1,530

Lottery

Pools

Betting Duty

Gaming

Amusement Machines

Bingo

93-94   94-95   95-96   96-97   97-98   98-99

Financial years

Source: HM Customs and Excise

Note 1. All figures have been adjusted to 1998-99 values.

Estimated net expenditure on gambling in 1998-99

Figure 4b

In 1998-99, net stakes[1] of some £7 billion was bet on activities subject to gambling duties

£ million

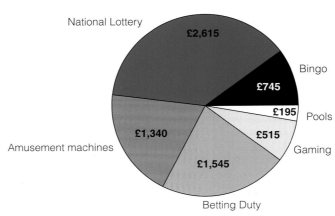

National Lottery   £2,615

Bingo   £745

Pools   £195

Gaming   £515

Betting Duty   £1,545

Amusement machines   £1,340

Note 1.   Net stakes = stakes placed less winnings.

2.   The estimated gross expenditure on gambling in 1998-99, and on which gambling duties would have been charged, is estimated at some £42 billion. This takes account of winnings which have been gambled again. (See Appendix B).

3.   Not all gambling is subject to gambling duties. For example, the following are exempt: on-course betting on horse racing; and local lotteries for charitable purposes.

Source: HM Customs and Excise

b) pools duty has fallen by 82 per cent in real terms. This is mainly due to the effects of the National Lottery coupled with reductions in duty rates, which have fallen from 37.5 per cent in 1994 to the present rate of 17.5 per cent (since 1998-99); and

c) general betting duty receipts have reduced by 15 per cent in real terms. These receipts have also felt the impact of the introduction of the National Lottery and there was a reduction in duty rates in 1996 from 7.75 per cent to the present 6.75 per cent.

Developments in offshore electronic betting and gaming

1.8 Two developments could affect substantially the future amounts of revenue that the Department collect from betting and gaming duties. These are the placing of telephone bets through bookmakers that are based offshore and betting and gaming provided on the Internet.

1.9 In 1999, a major UK bookmaker set up operations in Gibraltar to offer telephone betting to their customers, including those in the United Kingdom. Two other major bookmaking chains based in the United Kingdom have followed suit. Bookmakers operating from Gibralter taking bets only charge their customers 3 per cent compared to the 9 per cent which they charge in the UK. The UK charge consists of 6.75 per cent betting duty and 1.15 per cent horserace levy, with the balance being retained by the bookmaker. The Horserace and Betting Levy Board is also concerned at the impact offshore telephone betting may have on its revenues.

An example produced by the National Audit Office of how an internet web page might look

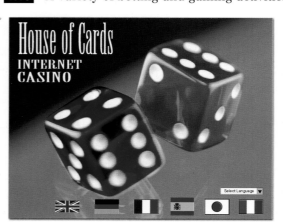

1.10 A variety of betting and gaming activities, such as virtual casinos, is now available on the Internet. The majority of these are based offshore and they are able to take bets from anywhere in the world by accepting credit card payments. Where the web site is based overseas, the operator is liable to pay any applicable duties in the country from which they are operating but not the country from which they are receiving the bets.

1.11 The Department estimate that lost revenue from telephone betting could amount to £50 million in 2000-01 if all telephone betting was to move offshore. Because betting and gaming on the Internet is still developing the Department estimate that the amount of revenue that is currently being lost is only small but they recognise it as a growing threat. The Department are currently devising a strategy to deal with these new developments and are taking part in discussions within the Organisation of Economic Cooperation and Development (OECD) to find ways in which member countries can respond to them.

What we did and how we did it

1.12 Against the above background and the Department's objectives (paragraph 1.2) we examined:

- the Department's analysis and management of risks to the revenue (Part 2); and

- whether the Department's arrangements for deploying their resources are fully effective in meeting the risks (Part 3).

1.13 Details of the methods we used are set out in Appendix C. In summary:

a) we conducted a questionnaire survey of 13 collections to obtain information on the way they administered betting and gaming duty work and to identify the data they use to monitor progress and performance;

b) we visited the Headquarters and nine collections to obtain information on the Department's approach to auditing betting and gaming traders and new initiatives that are being developed;

c) our consultants AEA Technology, Risk Solutions reviewed the Department's approach to assessing the risk of traders underpaying duties and allocating staff resources;

d) we sought the views of a number of third parties involved in the gaming industry, including trade associations and a selection of firms in the sector; and

e) we co-ordinated our work with that of our team carrying out a study on the Gaming Board to compare findings and identify areas where there was scope for closer working between the Department and the Board.

Part 2: The Department's analysis and management of risks to the revenue

2.1 The Department are responsible for assessing whether traders have paid the correct amount of duty and for detecting and deterring illegal traders who are seeking to evade duties. Our questionnaire asked the 13 collections on which betting and gaming duties the risks to the revenue are highest. Analysis of the responses shows that:

a) operators using amusement machines without obtaining licences were cited by eleven collections;

b) illegal bookmakers operating in pubs and clubs were mentioned by ten collections; and

c) of the other duties two collections cited bingo and four cited illegal gaming (casinos) as potential risks.

2.2 This part examines:

■ the ways collections dealt with the main perceived risks to the revenue - amusement machines without licences and illegal bookmakers; and

■ whether the Department could improve their intelligence on illegal traders generally.

Collections could take further action to ensure that new traders have registered

2.3 Under the Betting and Gaming Acts clerks to local licensing authorities are required to notify the Department of all licence or permit applications by betting and gaming traders and the date of any hearings to authorise these applications (Figure 5). The clerks for the licensing authority should subsequently notify the Department of which permits have been granted. Therefore, with the exception of trader applications to operate amusement machines, the main way by which the Department becomes aware of a new trader undertaking betting and gaming activities is through the local licensing authorities.

Figure 5

Registration procedures for betting and gaming traders

Trader	Local licensing authority	Customs and Excise
		HM CUSTOMS AND EXCISE

Applies for local Licence/Permit

Clerk notifies the Department of the application and date of the hearing[1]

Log details and investigate any intelligence the Department may have about the applicants

Licence/permit Hearing

Notify successful applicants and the Department

Receive Licence/permit to trade

Reconcile successful applicants with log and issue registration documents to trader

Complete Customs and Excise registration details 7 to 14 days prior to trading[2]

Reconcile details with log and allocate registration number to trader.
Add trader to local records.
Notify Accounting Centre at Greenock of new registration details.
Inform traders of details

Receive registration details and duty returns from the Department

Note: 1. Exceptionally, local authorities are not required to notify the HM Customs and Excise of trader applications to operate amusement machines.

2. Amusement machine operators apply for their duty licenses direct to the Accounting Centre at Greenock

Source: HM Customs and Excise and the National Audit Office

2.4   As there are over 1,000 licensing authorities in the United Kingdom giving an average of almost 77 licensing authorities for each collection, there is a risk that these licensing authorities may be uncertain to which of the Department's 13 collections they should report details of new traders. This is particularly the case where there are boundary differences between the licensing authorities and the Department. A licensing authority may, therefore, not always inform a collection of all new traders and the situation may not be detected by the collection.

2.5   The Department have considered whether to make the task more straightforward for licensing authorities by setting up a central point for all notifications. They have decided however that the centralisation of the task would not be the best use of resources as collections are better placed to gather and use the information.

2.6   The fact that a licensing authority has details of a trader does not always mean that the trader should have registered with the Department as there are traders who are not required to pay betting and gaming duties on their activities. For example a social club is not liable to pay duty on bingo if the revenue derived from it is not the primary source of income. Where circumstances change, a trader who originally did not need to register may need to. In our questionnaire survey of the 13 collections, one collection stated that they are planning to visit a number of such clubs in their area to ensure that the exemptions for not registering and paying duties continue to apply. The Department consider that this is good practice and intend to advise collections of the need to carry out suitable checks on exempt organisations where it is deemed appropriate.

2.7   From the response to our questionnaire survey and visits to collections we identified four collections that had carried out checks on the records held by local licensing authorities. For example, in February 1999, one of the collections contacted the licensing authorities within their area to obtain lists from them of all bookmakers, which they compared with the details on the registers. No illegal traders were found from this exercise but the collection gained assurance that the arrangements between themselves and the licensing authorities were operating as intended.

The Department are working to ensure that their information on traders is up to date and accurate

2.8   The Department consider it important that all data on traders on their registers is accurate and up to date. In cases where collections have been concerned about the accuracy of the data, the Department have carried out special exercises. For example, in response to concerns about the data on general betting traders and bingo the Department have reviewed and corrected the detailed data held on traders at the accounting centre at Greenock.

2.9   In response to our questionnaire, five collections stated that they were concerned about the accuracy of the data on amusement machines and licence holders held on the accounting system. They report having found that the licence holders' names and addresses and the types of machine for which the licences were purchased have been incorrect, and the accounting records have not been up to date on the duty paid by licence holders. In response to these concerns the Department are continuing with actions to improve the accuracy of the data.

The Department have difficulties in ensuring that all amusement machines are properly licensed

---

Amusement machine licence duty - risks to revenue

Traders may underpay the amount of amusement machine licence duty due by, for example:

- Only licensing some of their machines. On an unannounced visit to a trader officers found that only two out of three amusement machines had a licence. Other sites owned by the trader were also visited and the same situation was found. The Department collected £275,000 in licence duty, including £92,000 in penalties.

- Intermittently licensing machines, whilst continuing to operate them. A club purchased intermittently one month licences for each of their amusement machines but continued to operate them for a 14 month period. The Department collected licence duty of some £1,300.

- Purchasing a licence for a lower band of duty than that applicable to the machine.

- Operating machines without first obtaining a licence.

2.10   The Department recognise that there is a risk that they may not be aware of all permitted sites or operators and that consequently duty on some amusement machines may not be collected. This is because the Department have two key difficulties in ensuring that amusement machines have licences. First is the scale of the task as there are over 200,000 machines where the licence can be purchased either by one of 850 suppliers or major operators, or by over 60,000 small operators of the machines. Second, unlike other betting and gaming duties there is no statutory requirement for licensing authorities to notify the Department of traders eligible to pay the licence duty.

2.11 Collections have usually sought to detect amusement machines being operated without licences by undertaking drives either by location, such as a particular town centre, or by type of establishment, such as fish and chip shops. The announcement of a drive in the local press often prompts traders to obtain licences.

2.12 Amounts played through amusement machines are liable to VAT. Departmental guidelines advise VAT officers to check licenses or supplier details during their audit visits but we found that this was not always done. The benefits of these checks are:

■ disruption to traders is minimised;

■ betting and gaming teams are provided with additional intelligence; and

■ the scope or need for betting and gaming teams to perform their own drives is reduced yet gives greater coverage at minimum cost.

Specimen of an amusement machine licence

Specimen Licences

Amusement Machine Licence (Seasonal)

The original of this Licence must be displayed in a prominent position on the licensed premises

SPECIMEN

Address to which the licence was sent   Address of licensed premises

1. Licence number   Supersedes

2. Effective date   Expiry date

3. Number and type of machines authorised and total duty paid on this licence

Machines that are not gaming machines	
Small-prize (AWP) gaming machines	
Other (jackpot) gaming machines - lower rate	
Other (jackpot) gaming machines - higher rate	
TOTAL DUTY PAID £	

I hereby grant licence under Section 21(1)(a) of the Betting and Gaming Duties Act 1981 for the provision on the premises specified above of amusement machines of the numbers and description shown above.

Issued by the:

Greenock Accounting Centre,
Custom House,
Custom House Quay,
Greenock PA15 1EQ

Warning:- Providing unlicensed amusement machines for play is an offence for which there are heavy penalties. This licence does not authorise anything that would be unlawful under the social law.

Changes in regulations could improve the Department's ability to collect amusement machine licence duty

2.13 Legislation is silent as to whether the supplier or the operator of an amusement machine purchases the licence. The Department's data on the accounting centre at Greenock, therefore, holds details of the licence holder, who might be either the supplier or operator. The Department recognise that their ability to ensure that a licence is purchased would be improved if the record always noted both the supplier and the operator of the machine. They intend to include both sets of information on their records.

2.14 The Department recognise that there may be some benefits if amusement machine suppliers, of which there are 850, were made responsible for purchasing the licenses. This would, however, require changes to the legislation.

Amusement machines confiscated by the Department

Photograph by Rob Stratton

2.15 From 1995-96 to 1998-99, there were 18 cases where the Department took criminal action with respect to unlicensed amusement machines and 74 civil prosecutions. In addition 841 machines were seized leading to £206,000 of restitution receipts. Although there is no requirement on amusement machines operators to pay arrears of duties on machines for periods of illegal operation, action by the Department was nevertheless successful in collecting duty of £380,000 or £4,130 per case (Figure 6).

Outcome of cases where criminal or civil proceedings have been taken against unregistered amusement machines traders from 1995-96 to 1998-99

Figure 6	No of Cases	Duty
Criminal Proceedings		
Out of Court Settlement	18	£269,200
Civil Proceedings		
Prosecutions	74	£110,940
Total	**92**	**£380,140**
	No of Machines	**Restitution Receipts**
Seizure of Assets	**841**	**£206,000**

Source: HM Customs and Excise and the National Audit Office

Collections have worked with the Gaming Board and the police to identify amusement machines being operated without licences.

Two cases where collections worked successfully with the police and The Gaming Board:

- One collection believed that amusement machines were being used without licences on taxi operators premises. Working with the Gaming Board the collection sent a questionnaire to all taxi operators in their area asking them for details of the amusement machines used on their premises and used the responses from these to compare with the Department's data. The collection's staff also visited those operators who failed to respond and seized any unlicensed machines that they found on the premises.

- In a joint operation with the Gaming Board and the police, one collection raided a large number of premises where they believed amusement machines were being used without licences. As a result of this operation the Department collected £353,000 in duty and penalties from traders.

2.16 If the Department finds that a supplier is not ensuring that amusement machine licences are being purchased they may pass the information to the Gaming Board. For a supplier to obtain and maintain their Gaming Board certificate they must demonstrate that they are "fit and proper". The Gaming Board take into account the licensing of machines and will consider withdrawing certificates to trade from any supplier that incurs civil or criminal penalties.

2.17 The Department are currently seeking to improve their arrangements for sharing information with the Gaming Board. Our work confirmed that there is scope for the Department to work more closely with the Gaming Board, to tighten controls. This is because the Gaming Board expect amusement machine suppliers who are certified by them to keep photocopies of the licences for each machine, which they inspect during a visit. Based on information supplied by the Gaming Board, the Department could verify that duty has been paid on a sample of cases.

Action to deter illegal bookmaking is being taken both by the Department and by registered traders

Actions to detect illegal and undeclared bookmaking:

- Test betting to detect illegal bookmakers:

  The Department use test betting to confirm that an individual is taking bets illegally. This normally involves the placing of nominal bets with the individual to enable officers to observe the illegal trading activity. Before undertaking test betting the officer must have a letter of authority from the Head of the collection which sets out the officer's name, the place where test bets are to be made and the date on which the test bets are to be made. The written authority provides the officer with immunity against prosecution for participating in illegal betting.

- Action taken by the Department regarding on-course bookmakers accepting telephone bets without being registered:

  One collection had written to all on course bookmakers in their area inviting them to register if they were taking off course bets. Although one off course bookmaker registered, they have subsequently deregistered.

- Action taken by one company to deal with illegal bookmakers

  One major registered trader offered a reward of £1,000 to their betting shops if they identified an illegal bookmaker, subsequently leading to a successful prosecution. The Company were unable to measure the general impact that illegal operators have on their turnover but they cited one case where an illegal bookmaker was operating from a public house, such that, in their view, no registered bookmaker was able to operate profitably within a six mile radius.

2.18 While off-course betting is subject to betting duty of 6.75 per cent there is no duty payable on bets made on course with a bookmaker, unless made by telephone. The Department are aware that some on course bookmakers accept telephone bets from customers but do not register with the Department to pay duties. The Department have yet to collect any duty from such bets.

On course bookmakers at a race meeting who are not subject to duty unless they receive a telephone bet from a customer

Photograph by Gerry Cranham

2.19 Legal proceedings are expensive to pursue and before determining a course of legal action the Department will have regard to a number of factors. These may include the intention of the person(s) to evade duty and the amount of lost duty involved. From 1995-96 to 1998-99 there were 26 cases where the Department took criminal proceedings against illegal bookmakers and 15 cases of civil proceedings. The rate of return for investigations into illegal bookmaking was relatively low with total duty charged amounting to £175,000, an average of £4,300 per case (Figure 7).

Outcome of cases where criminal or civil proceedings have been taken against unregistered bookmakers from 1995-96 to 1998-99

Figure 7

	No of Cases	Duty and Penalty
Criminal Proceedings		
Prosecutions	10	£62,200
Out of Court Settlement	16	£65,100
Civil Proceedings		
Prosecutions	15	£48,100
Total	**41**	**£175,400**

Source: HM Customs and Excise and the National Audit Office

2.20 Where the major bookmakers find an illegal bookmaker operating in a public house they prosecute the landlord for failing to comply with the terms of his license and effectively deprive the landlord of their livelihood. Two major bookmakers have successfully prosecuted three landlords, and are pursuing a further case through the courts. At the time of our fieldwork they were conducting investigations in a further six cases and some seventeen other cases were in the pipeline.

The Department could improve their intelligence on illegal traders

2.21 There is only a limited amount of information available within the Department that might alert officers to the probability of illegal trading and they rely mainly on intelligence to identify the possibility of its occurrence. Three cost-effective ways by which the Department obtains information on potential illegal traders are:

■ through the use of hot lines;

■ contacts with registered traders; and

■ sharing information with other public sector organisations who have an interest in the activities of illegal traders.

2.22 The Department have a single Freephone hot line number **0800 595 000** which individuals or organisations can use to provide information in confidence on alleged illegal activity. In 1998-99, the Department received a total of 81 calls related to illegal betting and gaming, which was an increase of 10% on the previous year for allegations of illegal trading. Currently, the Department are investigating 15 cases of illegal trading on betting and gaming referred to them through the hot line. In 1999 the Department evaluated the use of the hot line and found that it has provided them with some valuable information.

Advert for HM Customs and Excise in a local telephone directory including details of their hotline number

2.23 We looked at how widely the Department publish the hot line number and its purpose by examining ten local telephone directories, ten Yellow Pages and the Department's Internet web site. We found that the hot line number was published within display advertisements for HM Customs and Excise in local directories but not within any of the Yellow Pages examined. Due to the cost of advertising space in the numerous local directories, the Department have confined the advertising of the hotline to report illegal activities concerned with drug smuggling and VAT evasion. The Department are considering however, the possibility of including more information in the directories but this will depend on whether it will be cost effective to do so.

2.24 The Department's Internet web site gives details of the hot line which can be used to report illegal betting but it does not mention other forms of illegal gambling such as illegal casinos. It sets out the reasons illegal betting is an important matter, the penalties for illegal betting and the type of information that would be helpful to the Department (times, places, dates, names and/or descriptions).

2.25 Collections' contacts with registered traders can also assist them with obtaining information on illegal traders. A registered trader is likely to detect quickly an illegal trader within their area because of the effect on their own takings. Trade representatives and large betting and gaming traders mentioned to us that they considered that the Department treated as low priority the pursuit of illegal betting and gaming traders. As a consequence major bookmakers have introduced their own teams to detect illegal bookmakers, usually operating in premises, such as public houses, which are not licensed for gaming (paragraph 2.21).

2.26 Collections have occasionally obtained information from the police, the Gaming Board and the Inland Revenue (making use of the statutory provision allowing HM Customs and Excise to obtain information from the Inland Revenue to assist with their duties). This information has helped the Department increase their understanding of the risks of illegal trading in their areas. In response to our questionnaire:

a) one collection said that they used information from the Inland Revenue to identify individuals who described themselves as professional gamblers and who could be operating illegal betting and gaming operations; and

b) another collection said that they held regular quarterly meetings with their local police and the Gaming Board to add to their intelligence information on illegal traders.

The Department consider that it would be difficult to set up central arrangements with the police service because of the number of police authorities, and therefore consider that it should be left to individual collections.

2.27 We recommend that the Department should:

In maintaining information on traders who should be registered

- remind collections to check on a regular basis the records of licensing authorities on new traders against the Department's records and ensure that their guidelines advise on how the checks can be carried out;

- set up a procedure for collections to notify Greenock (where receipts from betting and gaming duties are collected and accounted for) of inaccuracies in trader records to enable them to quantify the problem and allow causes to be identified and addressed.

With respect to the risks to amusement machine licence revenue

- look at whether they can use suppliers records to check that amusement machine licences have been purchased;

- continue to work with the Gaming Board to look at ways in which they can ensure suppliers check that amusement machine licences are purchased;

- pass suppliers' details to the Gaming Board where they find that suppliers are not carrying out their duties to ensure that licences have been purchased for their machines;

- ensure that the Department's accounting record for amusement machine licences issued includes information on the supplier of each amusement machine as well as the licence which would assist in confirming whether a licence has been purchased;

- consider seeking changes to the legislation to make amusement machine suppliers solely responsible for purchasing the licence;

- remind VAT officers carrying out VAT audits of the Departmental guidance on the opportunity for checking whether amusement machines are licensed when they come across them on a traders premises;

- look at whether they should pursue amusement machine operators for arrears of duties during periods of illegal operation.

With respect to the risks to revenue from illegal bookmaking

- encourage the provision of information by registered traders on illegal bookmaking;

- in assessing risk across excise duties, ensure that they still pursue sufficient cases of illegal bookmaking in order to maintain the integrity of the duty;

To improve their intelligence on illegal traders:

- consider the cost and benefits of better publicity for their hot line for example by including more information on its use in local telephone directories and on the Customs and Excise web site;

- look at whether there are further opportunities to share information on illegal traders with registered traders and public sector organisations such as the Gaming Board, the Inland Revenue and the police.

Part 3: Deploying resources to meet the risks to revenue

3.1 In this Part, we examined whether there are risks that:

■ Staff effort is misdirected into auditing traders who do not present the highest risks to the revenue;

■ The Department's targets on gambling duties do not adequately reflect their objectives;

■ Good practice to ensure that traders pay the correct amount of duties is not applied widely within the Department.

The Department are developing appropriate methods to identify risks and allocate resources

3.2 The Department allocate staff resources to collections for the audit of traders paying excise duties generally, rather than specifically for the audit of betting and gaming duties. Collections themselves decide how to allocate staff to the audit of individual traders taking account of local circumstances. In 1998-99, total staff resources for excise duties were 1,400 staff years. Of this total, collections allocated nearly 41 staff years to the audit of betting and gaming traders at a cost of £1.4 million.

3.3 We looked at:

■ how the Department identifies risks and allocates resources to the collections;

■ how collections then prioritise their workload and allocate the staff resources to the audit of traders paying betting and gaming duties; and

■ whether the Department could apply, more widely, existing good practices.

3.4 Up to 1999-2000 collections prepared annual bids for Excise staff resources, including betting and gaming, based on an informed estimate of risk. The Department allocated staff to them on the basis of a national overview of those bids. Compared with their risk assessment system for VAT traders the Department recognised that this approach did not adequately identify each collection's share of the risks. To address this, in December 1997 the Department started work on developing a system for international trade and excise duties, including betting and gaming which will assist them in allocating resources according to the risks (Figure 8). The new system will be introduced from 2000-2001.

Figure 8

The approach used by the Department to assess risks

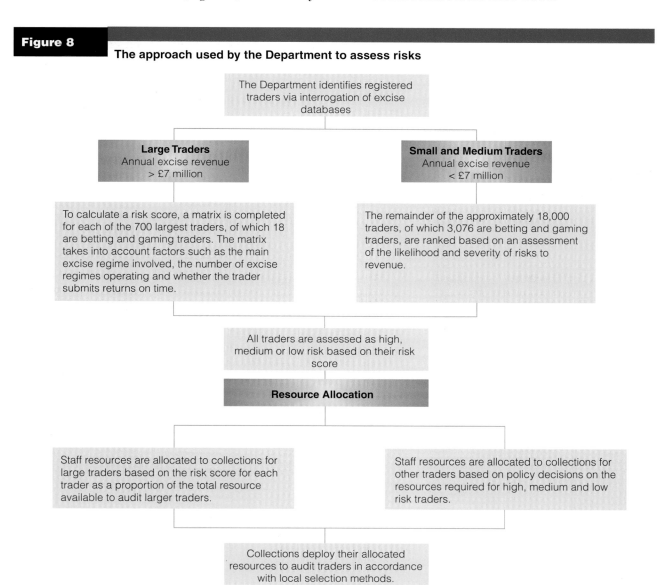

The Department identifies registered traders via interrogation of excise databases

Large Traders
Annual excise revenue
> £7 million

Small and Medium Traders
Annual excise revenue
< £7 million

To calculate a risk score, a matrix is completed for each of the 700 largest traders, of which 18 are betting and gaming traders. The matrix takes into account factors such as the main excise regime involved, the number of excise regimes operating and whether the trader submits returns on time.

The remainder of the approximately 18,000 traders, of which 3,076 are betting and gaming traders, are ranked based on an assessment of the likelihood and severity of risks to revenue.

All traders are assessed as high, medium or low risk based on their risk score

Resource Allocation

Staff resources are allocated to collections for large traders based on the risk score for each trader as a proportion of the total resource available to audit larger traders.

Staff resources are allocated to collections for other traders based on policy decisions on the resources required for high, medium and low risk traders.

Collections deploy their allocated resources to audit traders in accordance with local selection methods.

Note: The approach excludes the majority of amusement machine operators where the amusement machines form a peripheral part of their main business such as public houses

Source: HM Customs and Excise and the National Audit Office

The Department are developing a scorecard system for assessing the largest excise traders which could be further refined

3.5 In their assessment of risk, the Department give particular attention to large traders because these traders present a higher concentration of risks to the revenue than the general trader population. For the largest 700 traders, whose annual revenue turnover exceeds £7 million, the Department are using the scorecard method for assessing risks (Figure 9). This method is appropriate where there is a single risk and a large number of individuals or organisations against which to assess that risk. It is widely used, for example, in the financial services sector to assess whether applicants are suitable to be given credit or loans. We consider that the Department's use of scorecards is appropriate to their circumstances and should enable them to determine where the risks of underpayment are highest amongst the largest traders.

3.6 In examining the use of the scorecard for large traders, we noted that the Department gives a weighted score to traders who pay one or more of a group of Excise duties. For example traders who pay any of the six betting and gaming duties attract a score of 1.3 on the scorecard (Figure 9). A common score for a group of duties may mean that individual duties are given insufficient weighting because of their higher ratio.

For small and medium traders, the Department are using a simplified risk assessment system

3.7 For the remainder of the approximately 18,000 excise traders the Department are developing a less complex approach by producing separate scores for:

- the likelihood of underpayment (how often the trader is likely to underpay); and

- the size of the underpayment (how much could be underpaid).

In early 1999, the Department constructed a common database for these traders, from information supplied by collections. The Department are using this data to identify amongst small and medium sized traders those who present the highest risks to the revenue (by multiplying likelihood and size of the underpayment for each trader). They will use the results to rank traders and, from April 2000, allocate staff resources to collections based on the aggregate values of the risks for traders in their area. At the time of our examination, the Department were still developing the approach to assessing the risks for small and medium traders and

Figure 9

Description of the score card method for large traders

The scorecard method involves the Department completing a "scorecard" consisting of 14 criteria, two of which are shown below, covering items such as stock turnover; the type, number and amount of duties paid; trader compliance history; system and accounting complexity and historical control. Each of the criteria is subdivided into three or five associated with which is a numerical score. A trader is assigned to whichever subdivisions apply. The scores in the subdivisions are then multiplied to produce a total, which represents the level of overall risk for that trader. All of the large traders are then ranked according to their score. For collections assurance work on large traders, the Department set aside a proportion of the staff resources available for Excise duty work and have allocated these to collections in 1999-2000 according to the aggregate level of larger trader risk in each collection. The extract from the score card below shows two of the 14 criteria used by the Department and how these have been subdivided. On the criterion covering the principal regime, a trader paying more than one of the main duties in the sub divisions will attract a number of scores which will affect their risk rating.

Criteria	For goods based regimes	For transaction based regimes	Factor
Throughput per month, such as stock rotations, removal transactions and import entries	<500	<5000	1.0
	500 – 1000	5000 – 10,000	1.2
	>1000	>10,000	1.3
Principal Regime	Distilleries		0.9
	Wine, Cider, Perry, Registered Excise Dealers and other revenue traders not specified below		1.2
	Breweries, Tobacco, Hydro carbon oil, Hydrocarbon oil reliefs, Warehousing	Betting and Gaming	1.3
	Customs Imports/ Exports, Inward Processing Relief, Drawback, Common Agricultural Policy, Customs Warehousing, other Customs Reliefs.		1.7
	Warehousing		2.0

Source: HM Customs and Excise

we were unable to examine the criteria and values to be used for the likelihood and size of under payment scores, or how the results will be used and updated. The Department could also apply the approach used for small and medium traders to all traders to ensure that they all have a common baseline which would help identify those large traders to be assessed using the more detailed scorecard.

The Department recognise the need to monitor the audit coverage of individual duties

3.8 The results of the risk assessment to date show that there are imbalances in the deployment of resources between collections and that it may be possible to reduce the numbers auditing excise traders, including betting and gaming and redeploy them to deal with other risks to the revenue. The Department intend to redistribute staff between collections gradually as they recognise that the risk assessment work needs to be refined based on further experience and more data.

3.9 The Department intend to select for audit a percentage of the traders from each risk category designated low, medium and high risk, and which will range from 25 percent to 100 percent of the traders. Teams within each collection will sift the traders selected and pass to assurance staff those traders they assess as being potentially non compliant. Because the Department's approach applies to all traders paying excise duties there are risks that individual duties such as betting and gaming could receive little attention if the traders paying these duties have not been selected for audit. The Department intend to monitor whether there has been sufficient audit coverage of individual duties within each financial year and will increase the coverage if necessary.

3.10 In the longer term, the Department intend to allocate resources based on the total risks to the revenue covering both excise duties and VAT. Individual duties such as betting and gaming will then have even less significance in revenue terms in the larger population and the Department recognise that they will need to consider carefully how they ensure the integrity of individual duties when allocating resources using their risk assessment methodology.

Collections prioritise their work to deploy staff resources

Examples of the methods currently used by collections to deploy staff to trader audits

- A risk model provides a risk "league table" for all Excise and Inland Customs traders in the collection. It uses a points based system to produce risk scores for traders. To arrive at the risk scores, the model takes account of a number of weighted factors. These include compliance history, regime complexity and integrity, trader complexity, number of operational sites, revenue throughput, time since last assurance visit, marketability of the trader's products, intelligence and local knowledge. The model lists traders by regime at local office level. Local offices use the lists and local knowledge to select traders to audit.

- The collection identifies traders to audit, using risk analysis and information received. Bookmakers are selected for audit on a risk basis using the Excise Operational Planning System which provides a list of high revenue value traders and the time since the last audit. The remaining bookmakers are prioritised according to revenue risk; to support this process factors such as local knowledge, information received and information from the Greenock Accounting Centre database are used.

- The collection's betting and gaming team holds a meeting prior to drawing up their annual plan. Using local knowledge and a number of factors such as duty returns and trader compliance, the team draws up a list of traders to audit.

3.11 Within the staff resources allocated, collections decide how they should be deployed to carry out assurance work on the various traders paying duties within their geographical area. Prior to 1998-99 collections allocated resources to assurance work based on an informed estimate of the risk of the trader underpaying duties. Since then, the collections have used a more analytical approach based on three models developed by Scotland, Central England and Wales collections. The models are similar to those developed by the Department to allocate staff resources across collections for assurance work on Excise duties.

3.12 In 1998-99, collections deployed some 41 staff years to audit and administration work on betting and gaming duties representing 3 per cent of the total staff allocated to Excise and inland customs duty work. Within the total staff resources on Excise and inland customs work, the percentage devoted to betting and gaming audit work in 1998-99 at each collection varied from 0.2 per cent to 7.2 per cent (Figure 10).

Figure 10			

The number of staff years each collection used for audit and administration of betting and gaming duties in 1998-99

Criteria	Staff Years		Percentage of staff deployed on Gambling duties
	Excise and Inland Customs	Betting and gaming	
South London and Thames	115	8.3	7.2%
Wales West and Borders	104	6.1	5.9%
London Central	69	2.7	3.9%
Thames Valley	186	6.7	3.6%
Anglia	86	2.8	3.3%
Central England	106	3.5	3.3%
Northern England	99	3.0	3.0%
South East England	52	1.2	2.3%
North West	138	2.6	1.8%
Scotland	226	3.3	1.4%
Eastern England	114	0.6	0.5%
Southern England	75	0.3	0.4%
Northern Ireland	29	0.1	0.2%
Total	**1,399**	**41**	**3.0%**

Source: HM Customs and Excise

3.13 Most of the staff resources on betting and gaming have been used to audit general betting traders and those who pay amusement licence duty as the collections consider that these are the duties which are at greatest risk of being underpaid by traders. Seventy per cent of the collections staff time devoted to betting and gaming was on general betting traders and 23 per cent was on auditing traders who pay amusement machine licence duty. These staff identified additional revenue of some £4 million in 1998-99, of which around 60 per cent was from general betting and some 25 per cent from amusement machine audits.

3.14 The Department recognise that when they introduce their new system for allocating staff to collections they will need to monitor how collections then allocate their staff to audit work. In particular the Department intend to assess the extent to which collections are focusing on the areas of highest risk suggested by the risk assessment exercise and whether the results from the risk assessment exercise are robust or whether other factors need to be taken into account.

Collections need to consider whether staff resources could be deployed more efficiently and effectively

3.15 The efficiency and effectiveness with which the audit of traders is carried out can be affected by the way collections organise their staff and the decision making process in the selection of visits to traders. There are two main approaches which collections use:-

■ dedicated, or centralised, teams; or

■ dispersed teams of officers.

3.16 We categorised each of the 13 collections as to whether they take the "centralised" or "dispersed" approach to the assurance of traders paying betting and gaming duties, identifying seven centralised and six dispersed, and compared staff resources and outputs. Our analysis indicates that, although the dispersed approach has a better success rate per individual visit, the effectiveness overall of the centralised approach is significantly greater (Figure 11). The introduction of sifting traders for audit from April 2000 will allow collections the opportunity to consider their assurance strategy and whether their staff resources are organised in the most efficient and effective way to carry out their work on betting and gaming duties.

	Staff deployed in collection	
	Centralised	**Dispersed**
Assurance activities per staff year	124	69
Assurance visits resulting in an error	1:5	1:4
Net error per assurance activity	£731	£972
£ net error detected per officer year	£90,648	£67,106

Indicator of the performance of centralised and dispersed teams for auditing betting and gaming duties in 1998-99

Figure 11

Source: HM Customs and Excise and the National Audit Office analysis

The Department is developing new methods to select which traders to audit

3.17 At present collections use differing methods for selecting traders, which the Department do not consider to be fully robust (paragraph 2.14). The Department are therefore developing new methods for selecting traders for audit, which will help focus collections staff resources on the less compliant traders paying excise duties. The methods will be similar to those used on VAT assurance work and draw on the trader data used by the central risk assessment exercise for excise duties to identify those traders representing the highest risk.

3.18 With the new methods for selecting traders, Central teams located in each collection will use local records, knowledge and expertise to sift the traders that have been initially selected by their risk scores. The sift team will pass on to assurance officers for audit only those traders whom they have assessed as being potentially non-compliant. The Department started pilot testing the new arrangements for excise duties in April 1999 by applying it to two regimes. The lessons learned will be incorporated in a new approach to be implemented from April 2000 for all Excise duties.

The Department need to develop further the targets they set to measure their performance

3.19 One of the Department's principal aims is to secure the revenue yield and we looked at whether their targets enable them to measure whether this has been achieved. We also looked at whether their targets measure the efficiency and effectiveness with which staff have carried out the audit of traders.

3.20 The Department set targets on the amount of revenue to be collected from all duties and produced separate forecasts for the amount of the revenue that they expect to realise from groups of duties such as betting and gaming. The forecasts are based on past performance, known future policy on duty rates and forecasts of the state of the economy. From this is inferred the additional revenue the Department expects to identify in their audit of traders. The forecasts, however, do not measure whether the Department have collected the correct amount of duties as they cannot know what traders should have paid in duties.

3.21 A new measure on capped net additional liability for excise duties or tax under-declared after netting off overpayments against underpayments was introduced from 1998-99. The purpose of the target is to give collections an incentive to audit those traders where the risk of underpaying excise duties is highest.

3.22 The measure, however, does not take into account the level of resource used compared to the under-declarations detected. If it did so, the Department would be able to assess whether collections have used the risk-based approach to focus staff resources on the highest risks. Taking into account changes in business conditions, trends in the data might show that the net errors or net undeclared revenue increased without an increase in staff resources or the existing target had been met with fewer resources. From April 2000 the Department intend to introduce a new measure which relates the level of resources used to the amount of additional liability discovered.

3.23 By specifying the target in terms of net additional liability, audit staff could potentially focus only on identifying underpayments of duty by traders as identifying overpayments will be netted off against the target making it harder to achieve. The Department consider that they guard against this by taking it into account when setting targets.

3.24 In 1999-2000 the Department have set targets for the first time on the number of illegal bookmakers to be detected. In total they expect collections to detect 13 illegal bookmakers, which is the same number as those detected by the Department in 1998-99. The Department intend to review the target in the light of further experience.

The Department could apply, more widely, existing good practice to ensure that traders pay the correct amount of duties

The Department provide guidance and training to staff on how to conduct audits on traders

3.25 We found that the Department provide staff with written guidance on each of the duties which includes information on how to undertake a systems based audit of traders systems, techniques which can be used to confirm that the correct amount of duty has been paid and good practice tips. Collections' staff working on betting and gaming duties also attend a one week training course on how to audit traders and there are also seminars held on auditing aspects of the duties.

3.26 The Centres of Operational Expertise also have a role in providing support to staff. They cover three of the betting and gaming duties (general betting, amusement machine licence duty and gaming duty). On our visits to collections, staff mentioned that, although the Centres are helpful in providing advice when contacted, they do not take a proactive approach in disseminating information and good practice. Three collections in response to our questionnaire survey also mentioned that there is a need for more information on good practice.

3.27 The Department have recently carried out a review of the roles and responsibilities of Centres of Operational Expertise for all duties, including betting and gaming duties. As a result the Department will set up one Centre covering all betting and gaming duties and they are considering whether there is more that the central Centre of Operational Expertise could do to identify and disseminate good practice.

3.28 Collections' staff can use data on traders held on the accounting system at Greenock to carry out initial checks on whether traders are paying the correct amount of duty, including general betting duty and amusement machine licence duty. Checks can include whether traders have been submitting regular returns to pay duties, comparing the duties paid by similar traders and whether traders have declared turnover levels below those needed to break-even. The information can be obtained by interrogating the accounting system using the Department's computer software but at the time of our visits to collections we noted that the ability of staff to use the software varied considerably and that at one collection they did not have access to the software. Since then, the Department have set up a training programme for staff in the use of the software.

3.29 There have been occasions where the centre of expertise have supported staff in the use of the software and there is scope to extend these arrangements. To fully exploit the data held on the accounting system at Greenock the Department could also consider employing a statistician or analyst in comparative data to develop more sophisticated credibility checks that staff could undertake.

To assist them in their audit of traders, the Department could share information more extensively with other public sector organisations

Other areas where increased co-operation could help to ensure that betting and gaming duty is collected.

- The Gaming Board monitors the financial performance of individual casinos on a monthly basis to ensure that gaming is fair and to identify casinos whose performance may be a cause for concern. This information could be used by the Department to help gain assurance about the duties paid by these traders.

- Inspectors from the Gaming Board visit bingo clubs three times a year to evaluate the calculation of prize funds and ensure that statutory limits on charges have been complied with. Board inspectors could record the clubs' aggregate duty payable by quarter since their previous visit and pass this information to the Department.

- There may be scope for the Department to share information with other organisations including the Horserace Betting Levy Board (the Levy Board) and the Horserace Totalisator Board (the Tote). The Levy Board, for example, has developed a model of the whole betting market where the main variables used include gross domestic product and unemployment. The Levy Board intend to use the data from the model to check how much bookmakers should have paid as Levy.

- For business planning purposes, the Horserace Totalisator Board (the Tote) prepares detailed budget forecasts of future turnover. One of the indicators the Tote uses to predict the amount of turnover is the consumer expenditure deflator, which provides an historic measure of leisure spend. The Tote supplies forecasts of turnover and levy yield to the Levy Board but not to the Department.

3.30 The Department recognises that sharing information with other organisations can be an efficient and effective way of supplementing the information they hold on a traders activities. Three collections on their own initiative have already worked with the Gaming Board and the Inland Revenue to share information. For example we noted that:

- one collection obtains information from the Inland Revenue on bookmakers who the Department have selected for audit to help confirm whether the traders have paid the correct amount of duty; and

■ a number of collections have obtained technical advice from the Gaming Board on amusement machines and have exchanged information on request.

3.31 In order to explore the opportunities for closer working and sharing of information we set up a joint meeting with representatives of the Department and the Gaming Board. Both parties considered that two-way secondments could help improve understanding of each other's roles and responsibilities and identify ways that they could work more closely together, and so reduce the burden on businesses. The Gaming Board and the Department now have a joint liaison committee to facilitate closer working. The Gaming Board has already obtained information from the Department on major operators who have fallen behind in paying gaming duty - failure to pay gaming duty may bring into question whether an operator is fit and proper. There could be other areas where the Department, the Gaming Board and other organisations could work more closely to share information (see box).

The Department provide traders with information, advice and regularly remind them of their responsibilities.

Three collections which have taken action to remind traders of their responsibilities

■ One collection, in conjunction with the police, the local authority, the TV Licensing Authority, the Gaming Board, the Benefits Agency and the Contributions Agency, (now part of the Inland Revenue), wrote to traders in an area stating that the agencies were concerned that the businesses were failing to comply with various laws including the Betting and Gaming Act.

■ Two collections visited all bookmakers in their area to explain their obligations and asked them to sign a letter or form to indicate that they understood the requirements.

3.32 While audit staff do not provide any assurance to the traders themselves, we noted that three collections have taken action to remind traders of their responsibilities to pay the correct amount of duties. These initiatives provided:

■ opportunities for traders to clarify areas of uncertainty;

■ reduced scope for traders to claim ignorance of the regulations if a subsequent visit detected additional revenue; and

■ possible increased compliance because of the interest the Department was taking in them (see box).

3.33 We recommend that the Department should:

In assessing risk

■ place the large traders in the national risk analysis in the same way as for small and medium enterprises; and

■ ensure that sufficient audit coverage is given to each individual duty in each financial year.

In setting targets

■ ensure that planned sample audits are carried out to provide an indication of the extent to which traders are paying the correct amount of duties and to test the sift process;

■ continue to set and review targets for the detection of illegal bookmakers as a result of investigation work.

In applying good practice more widely

■ consider whether collections have organised their staff resources in the most efficient and effective way to carry out the audit work on betting and gaming traders;

■ ensure that the Centre of Operational Expertise takes a proactive approach in disseminating information and good practice to staff;

■ arrange for staff to be given support in the use of the computer software to interrogate the data on the accounting centre at Greenock;

■ consider employing statistical expertise in interrogating the data on the accounting centre at Greenock;

■ look at whether they could develop further their arrangements for sharing information with other organisations including the Gaming Board, Horserace Betting Levy Board and the Tote which would assist them in the audit of traders;

■ look at whether more should be done to remind traders of their responsibilities to pay duties.

Appendix A
General conditions determining whether betting or gaming duties may be payable

Pool Betting Duty

A1   Pools betting duty is calculated at 17.5% on the amount staked by players after deduction of any element that may relate to charities or sports if these comply with agreed conditions. The duty is payable when a bet is not at fixed odds and in particular where:

- the prizes are decided by reference to the stakes paid or agreed to be paid;

- a prize can be split between all the winners;

- the prizes or the prize winners are, to any extent, at the discretion of the promoter or some other person;

- the prizes consist wholly or in part of something other than money;

- coupon bets offer stated odds for a choice of bets and are invited by the issue of a coupon, a blackboard list or newspaper advertisement. This type of bet is not usually made without such an invitation.

General Betting Duty

A2   General betting duty is a duty on the total amount of money staked on off course bets either with the bookmaker in the United Kingdom or the Horserace Totaliser Board. The rate of duty is 6.75% of money staked and is paid by bookmakers in the following circumstances:

Betting duty is collected on stakes placed with:

Betting Method	On course bookmaker	Off course bookmaker
Cash bets	No – when bet made on course	Yes
Telephone bets	Yes – excluding a bookmaker who is not present at the meeting but who is making a hedged or laid–off bet by way of business with a bookmaker who is present at the meeting.	Yes

Bingo Duty

A3   Bingo duty is payable at 10 percent of the total amount staked by players, ie the purchase price of the bingo cards. Where the value of prizes paid exceeds the amount staked after tax, additional tax is payable at 1/9 of the excess.

A4   Bingo duty is payable on all commercial bingo played on premises licensed for gaming by the local licensing authority. Other bingo (non commercial) is also liable for duty unless:

- the game is promoted by a members club eg miners', welfare institutes etc;

- small scale bingo played at travelling fairs and arcades;

- machine bingo which requires an amusement machine licence; or

- the stakes or the prize money is less than £500 on any one day or £1,500 in any week.

Gaming Duty

A5   The duty payable is based on the "gross gaming yield" of each premise. The gross gaming yield comprises the total stakes less players winnings where the club is the banker plus "table money" on games where the bank is shared by players.

A6 The duty is payable at:

Part of Gross Gaming Yield	Rate
The first £462,500	2 1/2 %
The next £1,027,500	121/2 %
The next £1,027,500	20%
The next £1,798,500	30%
The remainder	40%

A7 Gaming duty is chargeable on the following games or games essentially similar to them

Baccarat	Craps	Pontoon
Big six	Crown and Anchor	Punto Banco
Blackjack	Faro	French Roulette
Boule	Faro Bank	American Roulette
Chemin de Fer	Hazard	Trente et Quarante
Chuck-a-Luck	Poker Dice	Vingt-et-un
Wheel of Fortune	Casino Stud Poker	Super Pan 9

Amusement Machine Licences

A8 There are two types of licences issued by the Department, premises based licences issued for the premises on which the machine(s) are situated or special licences which are available for individual non gaming machines, (video, pinball machines) and small prize gaming machines. To qualify for a special licence the operator must hold a minimum of ten licensed machines at any one time. Premises based licences can be for any number of months between one and twelve. Special licences are only available for twelve month periods.

A9 A dutiable machine that is not available to be played does not require a licence. Some amusement machines are exempt from requiring a licence eg, children's rides; machines where the cost per play is not more than 2 pence; and machines with limited prizes, eg if successful having played once then the player gets a free go or their stake returned.

A10 The current licence bands are as follows:

Licence Bands

Non Gaming Machines	Small Amusement with Prizes machines	Other Jackpot machines	
Annual licence £250	*Annual licence £645*		*Annual licence £1,815*
Video machines and pin ball tables and prize video machines eg, quiz games with a cost per play exceeding 35 pence	Small prize gaming machines where the maximum payout per play does not exceed £15 in money or money's worth and cost per play is more than 5 pence	Other gaming machines (jackpots) where the cost per play is 5 pence or less and prize money exceeds £15 in money or money's worth	Jackpot gaming machines where the cost per play is greater than 5 pence and the prize exceeds £15 in money or money's worth.

Appendix B
Estimated gross and net stakes gambled in 1998-99

The gross stake reflects the fact that a significant amount of the money wagered is returned back to players in the form of winnings and these winnings are often wagered again. Net stakes is calculated as the amount wagered less any winnings and is a more realistic estimate of consumer expenditure on betting and gaming

	Gross stakes £m	Net stakes £m
Pool betting duty	265	195
General betting duty	7,110	1,545
Bingo	2,710	745
Gaming duty	19,770	515
Amusement Machine licence	7,105	1,340
National Lottery	5,230	2,615
Total	**42,190**	**6,955**

Appendix C
Audit approach and methodology

C1 **We visited the headquarters to interview managers and examine supporting documentation to obtain information on:**

- Objectives, targets and management information systems for betting and gaming duties;

- The methods used for assessing risks in betting and gaming and allocating staff resources to betting and gaming duties;

- advice, guidance and training provided to staff auditing traders.

C2 **We sent a questionnaire to each of the 13 collections, and made follow up visits to nine collections, to obtain information on:**

- Objectives, targets and management information systems on betting and gaming duties;

- The methods used for allocating staff resources, selecting traders for audit and for confirming that traders have paid the correct amount of duty;

- Good practices they have used in their work on auditing betting and gaming duties;

- The role of Centres of Operational Expertise and how well they are operating.

C3 **With the assistance of consultants, AEA Technology Plc, Risk Solutions, we reviewed the Department's work in developing a risk assessment methodology for Excise duties including betting and gaming.**

The consultants examined a range of potential risk management methods to see which if any could assist the Department in their work. They also reviewed the Department's methods and documentation. The consultants discussed the methods with the Department's staff including a workshop that brought together relevant expertise from across collections together with the Department's central policy and management consulting groups. A copy of the consultant's report was provided to the Department.

C4   **We visited organisations involved with betting and gaming to discuss key issues, views about the Department's approach and initiatives undertaken by these organisations.**

The organisations visited were:

- The Betting and Licensing Office who represent a large number of Bookmakers;

- The British Amusement and Catering Trade Association who represent a large proportion of the members in the Amusement Machine trade sector;

- The Horserace Totalisator Board (The Tote);

- William Hills;

- Rank Organisation in respect of Bingo and Casino businesses.

We are grateful for the assistance they provided to the study team.

C 5   **We co-ordinated our work with that of our team carrying out a study on The Gaming Board.**

The purpose of co-ordinating the work was to compare findings and identify areas where there is scope for closer working between the Department and The Board.

We also arranged a joint meeting with representatives of the Department and The Gaming Board to explore the opportunities for closer working and the sharing of information. The meeting included members of our two study teams, three senior staff from HM Customs and Excise with expertise on auditing traders paying betting and gaming duties and two Senior Inspectors from The Gaming Board.

Reports by the Comptroller and Auditor General, Session 1999-2000

The Comptroller and Auditor General has to date, in Session 1999-2000, presented to the House of Commons the following reports under Section 9 of the National Audit Act, 1983:

Printed in the UK for The Stationery Office on behalf of the
Controller of Her Majesty's Stationery Office
Dd.5067505, 3/00, 5673, Job No. TJ001045